# Keeping Chickens
## (and your sense of humour):
## a beginner's guide

LORRAINE COVERLEY

First published 2015
This edition published 2016
Copyright © Lorraine Coverley

ISBN: 1530900093
ISBN-13:978-1530900091

With grateful thanks to the ladies: Sally; Debbie, Debbie,

Margaret and Thelma, who were patient

and answered lots of inane questions ...


and the girls: Tuppence; Paxo; Lola;

Tonto; Kettle; Rowan; Xena; Erica;

Daisy; Beryl and Lottie

who weren't, and didn't ...

# CONTENTS

# INTRODUCTION

I think it might be my fault. I think the words, "You know - I quite fancy the idea of keeping a couple of chickens", may actually have been mine.

The chicken house was still a drawing on the back of an old envelope when the silliness started. My husband was planning something normal - a box, basically, but discussions gradually started to include architectural features: crenellations; Tudor beams; a small jacuzzi in the basement ... Within ten minutes the simple process of planning a home for four chickens had become as complex as the construction of the pyramids, except that the Ancient Egyptians didn't need too many nest-boxes.

Crenellations, though - they were tempting. It was such a wonderful image. We suddenly had the image of four chickens in camouflage, crouched behind the top of the chicken house roof, armed with AK47s and a flamethrower.

We'd decided not to have a cockerel - it would really annoy the neighbours (whereas a troop of armed hens in the back garden wouldn't be a problem at all, until the fences burned down). There'd be searchlights on the roof, stabbing their beams through the darkness of the vegetable plot and playing havoc with the local kids' bedtimes; the sound of air-raid sirens and the all clear; the military marching of four hens on guard duty; the call 'Present arms!'; the endless Vera Lynn records…

When the metaphorical smoke had cleared away, we were somehow committed to the idea of hen-keeping.

Several years later, this book is the result. It's full of genuinely helpful stuff, but I couldn't resist allowing a bit of the silliness through.

Sorry.

# CHAPTER ONE

## ACCOMMODATION

Ask anybody about keeping chickens in a back garden and most will immediately think of *The Good Life* and that pink henhouse. If you ask someone to picture what it would be like to keep a little flock of hens of their own they'll probably imagine chickens strolling around a picture-perfect garden, while pecking the grass, and wandering (once a day) into a pristine henhouse to lay a clean, fresh egg. Hmmm. Keeping chickens is a bit like the way a swan swims. The top is clean, white and graceful, but the submerged bit's pedalling like billy-o.

That's not to be off-putting, though. There are many times when you really *do* see your hens strolling contentedly around the garden, and there's something about collecting a basket of just-laid eggs that gives a genuine thrill (okay, so I'm a sad person). But if you're thinking of keeping chickens you need a bit of hard work, some basic pieces of kit – and a sense of humour.

First, though, before you do anything else, you should check that restrictive covenants on your title, or local byelaws, don't prevent you from keeping livestock in your garden. The neighbours have to be considered, as well, don't forget. Hens can still be a bit noisy sometimes (at least ours are – one of our friends appears to have totally silent chickens. I'm not sure where you buy those). If neighbours are likely to be annoyed by the clucking of hens you might want to let them have an occasional box of eggs, and you definitely won't want to keep a cockerel. If the neighbour has dogs, you need to be really sure that your perimeter fences are completely dog-proof.

## The House

The first obvious requirement for a flock of hens is a house to keep them in. Commercially produced houses are available in a wide variety and a quick trawl through internet land will show you most of them. There are some very good houses, in different sizes for different numbers of chickens, but generally speaking I'd only consider these if money were no object, though the plastic ones are much easier to clean (and cleaning becomes a major issue once your new des. res. is inhabited).

Some of these plastic houses come with a small run, but the operative word here is 'small'. Most people I've spoken to who went this route ended up either keeping their chickens in it all the time and feeling dreadful because the chickens seem to be too cramped, or letting them out all day and running the risk of depredations by foxes.

A cheap alternative to buying or building a house is to convert something else, like a shed. Don't even consider converting a greenhouse - the temperatures in a greenhouse would be intolerable in summer for the hens.

Converting a shed will, however, still involve a certain amount of expense and work. You will need to ensure that such a large space is warm enough for them in the winter, you will need to build at least two or three nest boxes, and you will have to create a pophole door for them. The biggest problem with converting a shed is that it's almost certain to be resting on the ground. Rats do love to burrow and have been known to gnaw through concrete. If they think there's a way of nesting underneath your henhouse they will, so an elevated house is really the best way to go. This gives any hopeful rodents in the area nowhere to hide in safety.

A lot of people find the cheapest solution is to build your own, which is what we did (well, what my husband did - I handed him bits of wood and made lots of tea.) At this stage it's important to think about how many hens you plan to keep, in order to give them enough room. By UK law you must have at least one nest for every seven hens, and with at least 15cm of perch space per hen, but for the benefit of your hens, you really do need to give them more room. We don't keep as many as seven hens with only one nest box, because this can lead to bullying and aggression.

A good cheap but tough wood to use on the outer shell of the house is ply. Use an exterior quality ply. It's strong, easily cut and shaped, but not too thick. You will need a front, with a cut out for the pophole door, a back, slightly shorter than the front, so that you have a sloped roof to help rainwater run off, two sides, a floor and roof. For the perch we used 45mm x 45mm planed wood and for the supporting brackets for the perch, which stop it moving about, some 19mm x 32mm. The nest boxes (at least two, for four to six chickens) were constructed out of plywood and we made them without a roof, as they would be covered by two perch boards my husband devised. These run beneath the perch, keeping droppings (mainly) in one place under the perch and it also acts as a roof for the nest boxes so they use less wood to make. The other wood requirements are two small rails running alongside the pophole door, to keep it in place.

*Basic framework*

*Front, floor, ventilation holes and perch supports in place and all joints sealed to prevent insects getting in.*

The framework was made out of 32mm x 44mm planed softwood, screwed together, and the joins were also glued, to seal the joint and prevent insects from getting into the inaccessible parts of the house.

The supports for the perch went on next. The perch must be removable, for easy cleaning, while being sturdy enough for several chickens to sleep on it without feeling they need a seatbelt on. The floor should then be screwed in place, then the sides, back and front.

*House sealed, painted and awaiting doors*

The house must have ventilation. It's tempting to think that the chickens will get cold in winter, especially when there's snow on the ground and you have to keep defrosting their water, but they will almost certainly be warmer in their little feather duvets that you are in a coat, hat and scarf, and without ventilation they will be ill, so make sure you create holes (covered in wire if necessary for security) running along the length of the back and front of the house. A through breeze is necessary and in summer they'll be very grateful for it.

Finally we put on the roof. The house was painted in wood preserver and the roof was painted with three coats of a tough, flexible membrane coating, like Roof Seal. It might feel like a good idea to put a layer of waterproof material over the top to protect the house from the elements, but this is a very bad idea: parasites like red mites would love this cosy protection and would be impossible to get at, so never add a covering to the house, even temporarily.

The pophole door at the front should be placed between wooden runners, so that it runs smoothly, with a stop at the bottom, so it stays in place when down. Drill a hole at the top of the pophole door to take a sturdy length of thick cord, to the other end of which you can attach a simple metal hook. The cord will run across the roof, down the back and then attach to the bottom of the house, or some fencing, to ensure that the door doesn't suddenly fall down onto one of your girls as she's moving into and out of the house. Alternatively just attach the cord to a point above the door. It all depends on the siting of the house and ease of access to the pophole door.

It's difficult to advise specific sizes of house, but for six to seven chickens we built a house with the following final dimensions: the house was 90cm high, 70cm from front to back and the overall size of the roof was 80cm x 170cm. The two nest boxes were 30cm square and over them are the two trays, which are 34cm off the floor, so just covering the tops of the boxes. The perch runs the width of the house, 10cm above the level of the trays. The nest boxes must be tucked away in the house, where it's quiet and dark.

We built four pillars roughly 450mm high out of bricks and mounted the house on top of them. This is vital to keep it out of harm's way, preventing rodents (and foxes) from getting too close. Underneath it also provides a rather useful place to put food and water, out of the worst of the weather, and finally it will help you when cleaning out the house, so you're not grubbing around on the floor, trying to get into it.

To let the girls up into the house you will also need a short ladder (they will cope with the rungs very well) or a ramp, with some wood pieces across it, so that in icy weather they can get a good grip. They will feel a lot safer going up into a house, than they will at ground level.

Once you've finished it's best, in the interests of keeping neighbours happy, to try to make sure that the entire chicken area looks as reasonable as possible; keeping it painted or screened will improve the look of your garden and those of your neighbours and, in the case of screening, may slightly dampen any noise.

## The Run

The run is something that can vary widely from one household to the next. It's all down to individual preferences and space availability. It also depends on whether you are around all day to keep an eye on them in the garden – and, perhaps, whether you are simply prepared to run the risk of foxes, in order to let your hens have free rein all day. Nowadays people generally feel happier giving their girls as much room as they can, and this is not just important for the flock's happiness and the owner's conscience: it has definite health benefits if they can have a little more room, because disease and parasites flourish in smaller areas, and bullying and aggression are more likely if they are kept too close together. At the same time, none of us has unlimited space, so the size of the run has to suit the garden.

Even if you only have a paved area for them, chickens can be kept here, provided you occasionally disinfect the area, but they will need somewhere to scratch and dust bathe, even if it's only a sort of sandpit arrangement (which must also occasionally be sieved to remove waste, dead feathers, etc. and replaced when needed).

If you have only a small garden and if you're buying a commercial plastic henhouse with its accompanying run, do be aware that you will probably need to re-site the run frequently. Chickens need to peck and scratch, and they can decimate an area of grass quite quickly. They also benefit from being moved around to help keep parasites at bay.

If you do have grass, and they are allowed out into the whole garden at any time, check your fences first, in case there's a hole anywhere they can squeeze through. I have had the dubious pleasure of asking a neighbour if I can have my chicken back, please, and that resulted in much running about with treats and bits of spare fencing, in a bid to corral her and get her back into our garden (the chicken, not the neighbour). Retrieving missing hens makes for a good workout, but unhappy neighbours!

One person I spoke to while researching this book keeps her largish flock (about 12) in a converted dog run, formerly occupied by two Alsatians (who had worked out that kipping indoors in front of the telly was more fun). Other people simply have a small fenced off enclosure and let their girls out into the garden all day long.

Others again build an enormous run, to keep them safe. This was the route we took, as we have foxes like other people have weeds (actually we have the weeds as well). We also have a sufficiently large garden to build a good-sized run, and the obvious place to put the run was in an area under two large trees. This is ideal for chickens, offering them protection from rain and snow in winter and sun in summer. The other advantage for us was that this was an area where we had not been able to persuade anything to grow, so it was pretty much unusable land, anyway.

We began with marking out an area roughly 8m x 2m and calculating where the post holes were to go. We used a total of 25

50mm x 75mm treated timber posts. These posts would support the fencing, so we dug them down to approximately 30 cm. Between each post hole we dug a narrow channel to take the bottom posts and the fencing wire. Simply taking the wire down to the ground is no good, because foxes can dig really well and it wouldn't take them long to pull the wire out and get underneath it.

*Fencing fed under the posts to be cemented in place*

The top of the run will also need to be fenced over, as foxes are good at climbing and jumping. If possible roof a part of the run with a wooden section, to give the girls more protection from the elements. In winter they'll be very grateful for somewhere to be out of direct rain or snow, and in summer it will give them protection from the hottest sunshine, but don't roof the whole thing, or they'll get no sun when they want it.

We ended up using a variety of fencing over several years, but plastic coated mesh proved to be the best, most durable, option. The wire sections need to be cemented into place along the channel beneath the bottom posts, which make it impossible to pull the wire out. After a stealth attack from a fox who managed to gnaw the wire over a succession of visits until he could get right in and kill one of our chickens, we also put a second layer of much thicker wire of a slightly different size right around the bottom section of the fence, which seems to have foiled any similar attempts.

All this sounds quite simple, but it is a lot of work, especially in our garden, which has earth the consistency of concrete. There were moments, while trying to squeeze in under the bottom branch of one of our trees, armed with twelve feet of intransigent wire fencing, and a mouthful of nails, and then realizing we'd left the hammer out on the lawn, when it was tempting to think about skipping some of the work, but it really is worth it in the long run.

*Outside perches are a must, but old tree branches are even better*

Somewhere in the run the chickens will appreciate one or two perches, so that they can sit out there and sleep if they wish, or just as a way of getting out of mud if the weather is bad. Ensure that both inside and outside perches have rounded tops, not squared off ones, as they need to grip the perch with their feet and a rounded surface won't hurt them. They will particularly appreciate old tree branches, which are perfect as perches, and these will also harbour insects, which makes life more interesting for the girls when they scratch about for them.

Finally, to give them extra protection for the seriously bad weather, we fixed a very large tarpaulin to a metal pole, so that we could roll the tarpaulin across the top of their enclosure for the winter and when the weather improves it can be rolled back out of the way.

An alternative, if you're feeling energetic, is to make the wooden roof sections of the run sloped, and put guttering along the edges, so that when the tarpaulin is across most of the rainwater will run straight off and perhaps even into a water butt. Unfortunately we weren't feeling that energetic, so we do have a certain amount of baling out of water from the top occasionally, after heavy rain or snow.

## Other Equipment

The rest of what you need is fairly small beer, compared to the exertion/expense of building or buying the house and the run. The girls will need grain: corn; pellets or what is called 'layers mash'. When the birds are small they'll be given the mash by the farmer or breeder. As the girls get older they will be transferred onto the pellets, which are exactly the same food, but in a different form. They will also need grit – usually oyster shell – and corn, and all of these can be mixed together *(see Feeding)*.

It's worth shopping about to check prices for feed. Pet shops do stock corn, mash, pellets and grit but it's usually in tiny bags and is incredibly expensive. Feed suppliers, garden centres that sell chickens and farms that sell poultry are all better options, but prices vary enormously.

Another really good buy is a large, thick, rigid plastic bin of the type you used to put out for the dustmen (only make it a new one, for obvious reasons). All the food and grit can be mixed and stored really easily in there, leaving no plastic bags or paper sacks for rodents to chew through. Occasionally you should move the bin, and check that nothing's been trying to get in, anyway.

*Vermin- and weather-proof feed bin*

Chickens like to eat and then drink straight away, so the water and food need to be together. It also means that the water will get very mucky very quickly, so don't use bowls (in any case they will almost certainly knock them over the second you put them down). Instead use food and water dispensers, in plastic or metal, which have a feeding or drinking section at the bottom and dispense more feed and water when the level drops. These are easily obtainable from large pet shops, garden centres, etc. and, of course, on line. If you have a large flock you're going to need more than one of the food and water dispensers.

*A metal feed dispenser and plastic gravity water dispenser. Chicken wire over the feed prevents the hens from scratching it all out of the feeder.*

The dispensers should be kept as clean as possible, though the chickens seem to make it their life's work to keep them messy. The water should be changed every day (more often in the depths of winter or the height of summer),  but getting into the habit of changing it frequently also ensures that you're checking that  the dispenser is still upright and full. Despite the fact that these dispensers are harder to knock over, our flock have still managed it sometimes.

The feed needs topping up every day or so, but don't leave spilled feed everywhere; it just attracts vermin. The food should be completely emptied out occasionally, and the feed dispenser disinfected and refilled.

It may also be worthwhile making a shallow box, to place the feed dispenser in. It keeps spilled grain to the box and doesn't let it spread all over the run, where it becomes available to passing vermin, and it's much easier to clean up each day. Make the dimensions of the box about 10cm bigger than the feeder all round, so there's plenty of room for the girls to get into the food comfortably, without allowing them to get their feet right in and scratch it absolutely everywhere.

*Sawdust, cleaning equipment and empty egg boxes: other equipment you will need*

You will also need clean, dry straw for the nest boxes and a plentiful supply of old newspaper, to line the areas of the house where you're going to have to clean up. Sawdust for the floor is an optional extra – some people don't bother with it.

One last thing you'll need is a plentiful supply of empty egg boxes, collected for you by friends and family, because they're all going to want new-laid fresh eggs!

# CHAPTER TWO

# WHICH CHICKENS?

## The Chicken or The Egg?

When we bought our first hens there was a great discussion about what their names were going to be. I have to admit we then called one of them 'Paxo', because we have a wicked sense of humour, but there was never any possibility of our really eating her. The truth is, you simply can't name a creature and then put it in a pie.

It seems a little premature to consider eating your chickens before you've even bought them, but in fact it's a vital thing to think about, because that decision determines which breeds of chicken you're going to buy.

It is believed that the number of 'backyard' chickens in the UK is, at time of publication, around the three million mark, owned by probably three-quarters of a million people. The greater majority of these do exactly what we did: keep the chickens as pets - pets which happen to produce eggs.

In fact, many chicken owners have already made the distinction between 'pets' and 'livestock' without knowing it, by going to a farm or a shop, and buying from a selection of breeds already dictated by the farmer or breeder.

There's a huge array of breeds available, some pure and some hybrids (created by crossing the pure breeds), but a good proportion of the chickens for sale will be hybrids, which are all good egg-layers - some can produce up to around 300 eggs a year - while being interesting to look at, and easy to deal with. In other words, buy these chickens and you've just bought 'pet' hens.

Of those I spoke to when researching this book, something like 80% kept their chickens as pets, and every one of those people had taken at least one of their chickens to the vet at some point, for problems ranging from impacted crops to moulting. Poultry vets do not come cheap and the expenditure of a reasonable sum of money at the vet's is a clear sign that that bird is definitely a pet. Some owners will also take their chickens to be put down if they became old and ill, in exactly the way you would with a cat or dog.

## Chickens for meat

If you do choose to buy birds destined to be eaten, you will at least have the satisfaction of knowing the bird has had a happy life and you will also know exactly what it's been fed, and the meat is far superior to any commercially mass-produced broilers.

The pure breeds are thought to make the finest table birds, but these can take up to ten months to grow sufficiently to reach a suitable weight. They are generally quite slow-moving and placid, since a bird which isn't likely to dash about too much will put on plenty of weight.

For a table bird the best breeds, that is, those specifically reared for eating, are:-

- Ixworth - this takes its name from Ixworth in Suffolk, and was created from White Orpington, White Sussex, White Minorca and various varieties of Indian Game, to breed a white skinned table bird. They will lay between 160 and 200 eggs a year.
- Cornish (Indian Game) – this was created to be the ultimate meat bird. It has a broad, well muscled body and is deceptively heavy but, despite this, Cornish need adequate protection during very cold weather as their feathers don't provide as much insulation as those of most other chickens. They also tend to need larger popholes to get through. They will only lay around 80 to 100 eggs a year.
- Hubbard – this bird produces well-textured meat and gives good results for smallholders and commercial growers.
- Sasso
- Cobb - Sasso and Cobb are modern, commercial breeds, but the flavour is probably not as good, because these grow incredibly fast, growing to slaughter weight in as little as 12 weeks. They also sometimes struggle to take advantage of free range facilities, because they can't move great distances. These are known as 'broilers'.

One of the first things to consider with 'livestock' birds, intended for the table, is that unless you intend to buy in eggs or chicks, you will need a cockerel in order to rear your own, keeping the females for future egg production and slaughtering the males. But there's nothing quite like a full-grown cockerel letting rip at dawn in a densely populated area to make you deeply unpopular with the neighbours, and this fact alone may account for the predominance of the 'pet' chicken over the livestock variety.

For table birds, your first decision will be whether to hatch your own chicks or buy day old birds. Economically Sasso or Cobb would be cheaper than breeding your own dual-purpose birds and rearing the cock birds for slaughter, but the flavour is perhaps the greatest issue here, and a dual-purpose, more slow growing bird will be far superior in taste. Though it's perfectly feasible to do this with bantam breeds, they are obviously not going to reach any sort of reasonable size, when compared with other breeds.

If you decide to hatch your own, and don't wish to have a cockerel on the premises, you can buy hatching eggs and put them under a broody hen or in an incubator, though perhaps only four out of six will probably hatch. That loss has to be built into the calculation when working out which way to go, particularly if you choose to use an incubator, which has to be heated, though the cost per day is fairly minimal.

On average the cost of raising a dual-purpose chick, say a Light Sussex, would be double that of raising a fast-growing broiler breed, but if you hatch perhaps 50% female chicks, those will go on to become your egg-layers, so this can be a very good method for those who need both eggs and meat.

The next expense is feed for the chicks, and, again, dual-purpose chicks will cost perhaps twice the consumption of a broiler, because they take longer to rear to slaughter weight. But if you compare final rearing costs to the cost of a shop-bought chicken, it's still pretty economical, if you're happy to put in the additional work.

The next question, though, is that of slaughter, which begs the question, could we kill a chicken? This can be a lot easier said than done. I have heard of people getting the vet to do this for meat birds, which makes the meat so expensive you might just as well buy laying hens instead, and pop down to the local butcher's for your free-range chicken.

Methods vary, but most people dislocate the necks of their birds, using a 'humane killer' device, or their hands, but some I spoke to dodged the issue entirely, by having a helpful neighbour do it for them. The main thing is that it's done humanely. It would be best to have somebody with a lot of experience demonstrate the method first, because it's definitely not something to 'have a go at' without practice and knowledge.

You should starve your chickens for 24 hours before you begin, as undigested food gets in the way of the butchering. The old method of pulling the neck, when done very firmly and decisively, is one of the most humane methods of killing them. This involves grasping the legs of the bird in one hand while grasping the top of the neck near the head with the other hand and pulling firmly in opposite directions until you hear a click, which is the sound of the neck bones coming apart. The bird may flap briefly and then stop moving, but if it has dilated pupils it is dead.

Plucking is best done while the bird is still warm, and will take about 20 minutes. Be careful not to rip the skin. Once plucked, begin dressing the bird by removing the head, then cut the neck away. Then carefully cut around the vent, ensuring that you don't cut into the intestine. This makes enough room to reach inside and 'draw it', i.e. remove the innards. Check that there is no offal left inside the bird, truss it with string to keep the legs and wings in place during cooking and either cook straight away or freeze.

## Chickens for eggs

You may prefer to take on some former battery hens, and give them a new lease of life. Ex battery hens are not, contrary to popular belief, unhealthy - just unfit. The British Hen Welfare

Trust is a very good first point of contact for advice on buying these and if you're buying battery hens, do buy them through a reputable charity, rather than direct from the farmer – after all, he's already made enough money out of them. In addition, they will have been checked over by the charity and if you need assistance they will be able to offer it.

If you are taking on former battery hens, to try to give them a better life, do be aware that they may need their feed in the form of crumbles, rather than pellets (*see Feeding)* and their behaviour will almost certainly be different from that of free-range hens, though watching them explore their new surroundings will be a great sight! Ex-battery hens will be rewarding to keep, and will probably still lay you a lot of eggs, because they will be hybrid breeds, i.e. good egg layers.

The following is a guide to some of the best egg layer breeds:-

- Amber Lee – a hybrid, which is a beautiful cream colour and lays around 330 brown eggs a year.
- Ancona – rather flighty birds, originally from Italy, with a greenish metallic sheen to their feathers. They lay around 180 small white or cream eggs a year (no, not that sort of cream egg!)
- Andalusian – originally from Spain, these bluish-black birds are a good back garden choice, which start laying very young. They will lay about 160 white eggs a year.
- Araucana – originally from Chile, with attractive blue-green colouring to the shells and about 180 eggs a year.
- Black Star – a hybrid from Holland. A very hardy bird, which comes in all sorts of colours from all black to black and copper and lays around 300 brown eggs a year.
- Bovan Goldline – a very friendly hybrid, which is ideal for children to keep, and lays around 330 brown eggs a year.
- Dutch Bantam – these little birds are quite hardy but do need to be protected from winter weather. They can fly quite well, so good fencing is a must, but they can become very attached to their owners. They are good layers but will only lay in the summer months, so they will lay fewer eggs, though it could be as many as 150 a year.

- Friesian – (not cows, these are definitely bantams) these are a very old Dutch breed, which produces around 220 white eggs a year
- Gingernut Ranger – this sounds like a biscuit, but is a very friendly hybrid, which is placid and inquisitive. They are excellent for children and love ranging around a garden, foraging, and lay up to 320 large brown eggs in a year.
- Lakenvelder – originally a German breed, these are quite small, but good layers, sometimes laying tinted eggs (but mainly white ones). These are pretty flighty and rather wild, so aren't as good for children to keep. These are mostly black and white, though some are blue and white and they will lay around 160 eggs a year.
- Legbar – these come in a variety of colours and will lay around 180 blue eggs a year.
- Leghorn – this is originally from Italy, and is another very hardy breed available in a number of varieties. They are, however, very noisy, so don't choose these if you have fussy neighbours, and they love to move about a lot, so they enjoy free-range foraging. These will also roost in trees, if given half a chance! These are not particularly tame, so in all respects are not well-suited as family pets, but will lay about 200 white eggs a year.
- Marsh Daisy – originally an English breed from Lancashire, this is a hardy hybrid in a range of brown colours, which lays tinted eggs; however the breed is currently considered endangered.
- Minorca – the largest Mediterranean breed, available in black, white, blue and bantams. They will lay around 170 white eggs a year.
- Rhode Island Red – a classic favourite, these are a good choice for the back garden owner. These birds are quiet, but alert and pretty hardy. They make good pets, and can cope with most conditions better than other breeds. They will lay about 180 brown eggs a year.
- Scots Grey – an old breed, from the 16th century, known for its ability to thrive in most climates, this is another breed that likes to roost in trees if it can and they do need

plenty of space, partly because it's a long-legged breed which is fond of foraging. These will lay about 170 eggs a year.

- Speckled Star – another hybrid, this is very docile and lays approximately 270 speckled chestnut brown eggs in a year. The most significant feature of the Speckled Star is its soft, silky plumage.
- Speckledy – another docile hybrid in colours from silver to dark grey, these lay more than 300 brown eggs a year
- White Star – a snow white hybrid that lays around 300 very white eggs a year.
- Welsummer – originally from Holland, these are another excellent back garden pet for children to handle and lay around 160 terracotta coloured eggs a year.

## Meat and Eggs (the dual-purpose breeds)

To a smallholder, or anyone seeking birds which can be reared to give females which lay a fair number of eggs, and males which can be slaughtered once they reach a given weight, it is dual-purpose breeds that are needed. Most of the good egg-laying breeds are comparatively light-bodied and just don't have enough meat on them to make it worthwhile eating them. Exceptions would be Orpingtons, Speckledy or Blubelle, which are both good layers and also good table birds. Generally, though, the dual-purpose breeds are a compromise, with lower egg production generally.

Some good dual-purpose breeds are as follows:-

- Australorp – developed in Australia these currently hold the egg production record, with 364 eggs in one year from one hen, but generally around the 200 mark.
- Barnevelder – originally from Holland, these are hardy and placid and will lay around 180 eggs a year.
- Bluebell (or Blubelle) – a hybrid in a variety of grey colours, these are very placid and will lay around 250 brown eggs a year.
- Brahma – a very heavy bird, very good-natured and good for children to keep. They lay around 140 eggs a year.

- Dorking – known for very good quality meat, this is one of the oldest breeds, first brought into Britain by the Romans. They are hardy, docile and active birds, who lay around 140 white eggs a year.
- Faverolle – originally from France, these gentle friendly birds are another good breed for children to keep, and lay around 160 tinted eggs a year.
- Houdan – another docile French breed, these like to be handled and can live for up to eight years. They lay around 160 large white eggs per year.
- Jersey Giant – as the name suggests, these are extremely heavy, but slow-growing birds, with very little meat until they are about six months old. They need plenty of space and lay around 180 brown eggs a year.
- La Fleche – flighty, active birds, which do not appreciate human contact, but produce around 200 white eggs a year, while their flesh is quite white and of good quality.
- Langshan – originating from China, these are mainly black and, unusually, even the cockerels are pretty docile. These intelligent, inquisitive birds lay pinkish-plum or cream coloured eggs – around 180 a year.
- Magpie – this black and white hybrid (see cover) was bred in France, creating a good egg layer, which is larger than a lot of other hybrids, with a very good temperament. On the small side for a table bird, it is nevertheless feasible as a dual-purpose, laying around 220 eggs a year.
- Maran – another French breed; easy to look after and pretty resistant to disease. Though they are generally placid, they are not always so and are best not kept around younger children. They will lay around 150 dark brown eggs a year.
- Naked Neck – originally from Hungary, these have half the number of feathers on most other breeds, making them very quick to pluck, but that does mean they need extra protection during colder months. They can be aggressive, and will lay around 100 or so brown eggs a year.
- Orpington – Black, Buff or White varieties, these are very large, docile birds, which are greedy, and lay relatively

small eggs (around 160 a year). Despite their size, they can be bullied by smaller breeds.

- Plymouth Rock – named after the town in America, not Britain, this is a popular breed, which is hardy, friendly and attractive, and lays around 180 cream or tinted eggs a year.
- Redcap – originally from Derbyshire, and mainly known only in that area, but this is one of our oldest dual-purpose breeds. These are said to have an excellent, gamey, flavour but require a lot of space, though they will lay around 150 to 200 eggs per year.
- Sussex – a classic dual-purpose bird, originating from the county of the same name, these are excellent birds, producing good quality meat, while the hens will lay around 200 – 250 brown eggs a year.
- Wyandotte – a medium-weight bird, and the hens make good mothers. These have a fairly good temperament and will lay about 180 eggs per year.

### Showing Birds

For some people a natural next move, once they're used to keeping chickens, is to start showing them. This does, however, involve breeding your own chicks, which starts to become a lot more complex and requires you to make choices from amongst the chicks to decide which will be the better birds to rear. This involves either having a cockerel or buying in eggs and rearing and hatching those.

The Poultry Club of Great Britain recommends pure breeds for showing and in fact, though some shows will include hybrid classes, this depends on the area where you live.

Light breeds, like Leghorns for example, can be pretty flighty, so a heavy breed may be best to start with, because they will obviously need to be handled a lot.

The very best way to start showing is to attend a few shows first, and talk to other breeders and owners.

# CHAPTER THREE

## SETTING UP AND STARTING OUT

### First Steps

So – how many do you buy? And how do you set them up in their new des. res. in your back garden? What, in short, can you expect?

The first essential is that you don't buy just one chicken. You will need at least two, for their benefit. If you're rehoming battery hens you'll find that you will probably be required to buy three, for company and comfort. A chicken needs company because it's a flock creature, and in winter it will need the extra warmth provided by cuddling up with other hen(s). Beyond that, the number you can have is limited by the size of the henhouse and run *(see Chapter 1)*. Also ensure that they are similar sized breeds, so that larger birds don't intimidate or injure smaller or timid ones. Remember, too, that just because a breed is large doesn't mean that it can't be bullied by smaller birds. Buff Orpingtons are a popular choice for a back garden, as they have a lovely temperament, but smaller, more aggressive breeds can intimidate an Orpington. Obviously, if you keep bantam breeds, you can't put physically larger birds in with them unless they are extremely good-natured.

If, when you are choosing your chickens, one crouches down as you approach it, this is a sign that it's happy to be stroked by you. It's a very good idea to try to choose birds like this, because they will be less stressed by handling and more friendly. A chicken that's happy to be around humans is far safer if you have children, too. You must, however, ensure that children don't snatch at the birds, or chase them. They need to learn what is appropriate behaviour around any creature, and hens are no exception.

It is useful to get the girls to allow you to handle them as much as possible because it makes trips to the vet, or treatments for problems, so much easier - not to mention less stressful for the chickens. It's good practice to make a point of trying to stroke them as often as possible, so they associate it with the pleasant sensation of being stroked and not with being grabbed. If you want to pick them up, make sure you have their wings safely tucked under your arm, so they can't flap and hurt themselves struggling. They should quieten if you hold them like this. Theory also has it that holding them upside down quiets them, but experiments in our back garden fail to support this.

Placing newspaper on the bottom of the house will make it easier to clean out later. Never put food and water inside the house – it will be tipped over almost immediately, and food inside the house will just encourage rodents. If wished you can put sawdust over the newspaper. Line the nest boxes with newspaper and add some straw, for the comfort of the hens and protection of the eggs from breaking.

When you bring your girls home for the first time put them into the house and close the door. They won't come to any harm just overnight without food, and will be all the more keen to leave the house the next day to find some. Locking them in like this calms them down after their journey and shows them where they now live so they can find it again the next day; otherwise they may become confused and not know where to go to sleep.

The following morning open up the pophole door and let them come out in their own good time. They may be reluctant to explore their new surroundings but hunger will eventually drive them out. To begin with make sure they stay in their run, so they learn that that, too, is theirs. If you let them straight out into the garden and they are panicked by anything they will scatter in all directions and you'll spend the day trying to retrieve them, which will be particularly difficult, as they won't know you.

Many people are unsure whether hens will lay without your having a cockerel. They certainly will. What they will be laying are unfertilized eggs. If you have a cockerel as well, you will have some fertilized eggs, which can be hatched to produce chicks to replace the older chickens. This is useful for someone who wants to eat the meat as well, but a cockerel is unnecessary for most back garden chicken keepers.

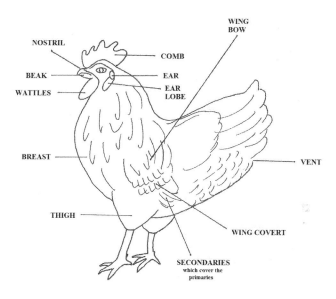

*Some of the parts of a hen are obvious, but others aren't*

If you buy in a point of lay bird the comb and wattles will be small and pink, but the comb will increase in size and when they are ready to start laying, you will notice the comb and wattles turn red. Our Magpie, Kettle, is on the cover of this book, and you will notice her bright red comb and wattles.

If you're re-homing battery hens, they may well have a pale, soft comb, because of the conditions they've been living in, but this will soon turn red. They also may not arrive with many feathers, but, again, they will soon start to grow them and within a few weeks they'll look like any other hen.

## The Eggs

The very first couple of eggs young birds lay may have soft shells or be odd sizes, but this will settle down within a few days. Depending on their laying rates you may see an egg laid every 26 – 28 hours. They won't actually lay an egg a day even if they are at

35

'full production', as they don't go by human timescales, so you'll find the number of eggs in the nest boxes may be three one day and four the next and only one the day after.

In any case the number of eggs laid by any chicken will vary. Some breeds lay more than others (see below). In winter many breeds lay far fewer, and less often, while some are unaffected by the weather. Most will stop laying while they moult, as all their energy is going into producing their new feathers. And, of course, if they're not well they may stop laying.

It's a very good idea to start as you mean to go on, by keeping records. When you first buy your chickens make an exact note of what breed they are, how old, where they came from, and when. If you have problems later, you can consult your records and speak to the farm or breeder who sold the birds to you. Equally, if you find a particular chicken is a real favourite, as long as you know what breed it is, you can buy another from the same source. It's amazing how quickly otherwise you forget the details.

It's also a good idea to make a note of how many eggs are laid each day. It only takes a second to do, but it allows you to spot potential problems early. If chickens go off lay it's much easier to notice this from egg numbers and pinpoint when it first started. There may be a fox prowling round, putting them off; there may be a problem with red mites or other parasites; or perhaps the weather is colder outside than you realized and they're beginning to focus on using their food to keep themselves warm, rather than laying eggs, and need more feed available. Keeping records makes it much easier to spot a trend and deal with it.

It's best to collect eggs on a daily basis. It's essential to prevent the chickens from eating the eggs themselves, and if they're lying in the nest box for a while the girls may break them accidentally and then get a taste for them.

When collecting the eggs you can leave them covered in mud and other stuff or you can wash them. Special egg wash products are available, but we just use a cloth and plain water. There is a theory that it is wrong to clean the eggs at all, because this removes the 'bloom' on the outer layer. The bloom is protecting the eggshell from bacteria getting in, but I never leave eggs unwashed, for two reasons. Firstly the bloom is only relevant if you intend to keep the eggs for a long while – and we never do. Our eggs never last longer than a week at the outside. Secondly, if I'm baking a cake and accidentally drop a piece of shell into the mixture I want to know that when I fish it out again I'm not leaving behind any foreign bodies in the bowl – and mud isn't the worst of it!

Whether or not you decide to wipe the shells, always pencil on them the date when they were laid, so you won't use them in the wrong order.

If you forget to put a date onto an egg, it's easy to tell whether or not it's fresh. As an egg ages, more air enters through the shell, creating more of a gap between the shell and the contents. A fresh egg, with very little air, will sink if placed in a bowl of water, while an older one will, of course, tend to float more.

The best way to keep eggs is not in the refrigerator, but in a crock at ambient temperatures. Fresh-laid eggs won't be hanging around for long, so they'll be perfectly safe, kept like this. In addition, boiling an egg that's been taken from the cooler temperature of a 'fridge will tend to make the eggshell break during cooking.

Incidentally, don't forget that these eggs won't be the regular, commercial sizes. If you're baking with them, the weight of the eggs (in their shells) is your guide to quantities for the other ingredients.

## Cleaning Out

The house should be cleaned out thoroughly at least once a week, or more often in hot weather, or if you have a large flock, which is creating more mess. Rubber gloves are an essential – it can be quite difficult to get the smell off your hands otherwise. Ensure the henhouse is empty, and that you're not disturbing one of the girls in the nest box. Close up the pop-hole door, or they'll all come in to help! Begin by taking out the nest boxes and changing the paper and straw. Pull out all the newspaper and sawdust from the floor and clear off any remaining waste and dispose of it (the chicken mess is particularly good for the compost heap, as long as you don't put it straight onto the garden for a few weeks and give it time to break down). Occasionally you should give outdoor perches a scrape down, and scrub them clean, and do this for the indoor perches every time you clean out the house boards. For these scraping jobs the best tool is an old wallpaper scraper.

*The house has newspaper and sawdust on the floor, two nest boxes*
*with straw inside and covered by boards to collect droppings. Above that is the*
*perch for night-time, with ventilation holes above.*

In hot weather try to clean the house out in the morning, so that you can scrub it with disinfectant and leave it open to dry in the sun. Periodically spray the interior of the house with a poultry insecticide and while it's still damp, apply some diatomaceous earth. This will stick to the perch and other parts of the house and if red mite or other parasites come into contact with it it will pierce their exoskeleton and allow the insecticide to kill them.

Once the house is clean (and dry, if you've done a complete scrub, disinfect and clean) put in fresh paper and sawdust and replace the cleaned nest boxes. You could put some sand onto the perch boards, to stop any pooh from sticking to the wood, or just line them with newspaper (though this can stick to the boards). Then you can open up the pophole door and let your by now impatient hens back in.

After a few seasons' worth of hot sun and freezing icy weather, the boards of a wooden house may well shrink and warp, causing some gaps that can let in draughts. Keep an eye out for these, especially in summer, when it's easier to deal with them by replacing boards or a section of the house. Don't use an extra piece of wood to cover over the gaps, though – these are ideal hidey-holes for insects. Unfortunately it will mean a proper overhaul of the house.

## Rodents

Be aware at all times of the existence of rodents. It's said that you're never more than ten feet from a rat, which is a chilling thought. Rats spread diseases, human as well as animal, and should *never* be tolerated. Don't ever delay calling the council: they would far rather you called out their pest controller to deal with just one rat, than your leaving it, because rats will breed if they're left alone. It may be that a rat is just passing, and is forced by bad weather to hang about for a time, and maybe it won't stick around because there is nowhere nearby to hide properly, but call the pest controller out anyway, to make sure. He or she will put traps down and will come back to check them.

If rodents *are* hanging around your chicken feed, they are more likely to be mice. A good idea is to set up an early warning system for rodents. Find an old deep bowl, perhaps a breakfast bowl, and put some feed in it. Smooth the feed down, so it presents a flattened surface. Put it near the chickens' area, but not right next to it. Use an old plastic box and place it over the bowl, propped up on a short stick. Any rodents in the area will go there first, because it's much easier to access than going to the feeder itself (chickens will catch and kill mice if they see them near their food).

Check under the box every couple of days. If you see that the surface is disturbed, or see droppings in or around it, you probably have a mouse. Old-fashioned wooden mouse traps are usually the best, but if you prefer to use humane traps, do be aware that you need to check every day at least, and release any mice a long, long way away, or they will be straight back.

Mice love chocolate and peanut butter, and these are the best

ways to bait traps. Peanut butter is particularly good, because it can't be snatched off by a rodent before the trap springs. It also, unfortunately, attracts slugs (at least, it does in our garden) and I understand from my husband, who does rodent patrol, that there is no manly way of cleaning a dead slug off a mouse trap without going, "Yeeuchh!"

## Foxes

We were solemnly assured by more than one person that male urine is a deterrent to foxes, and that all we (well, not me, obviously) need do was to take a stroll around the run late one night and have a wee and that this would stop them hanging round.

Try this if you wish (if nothing else, it should give someone a laugh) but personally I'd rather depend on good fencing. In winter, with snow on the ground, we always notice the pawmarks of the local fox, on a route past our chickens' run. He is checking that we haven't had some sort of mature moment and left the run open for him. It doesn't matter what the theories say; there *is* a fox around your garden and he or she is well aware of your defences. A fox can get into a run in a remarkably short space of time, and in total silence. One of our hens was once snatched mid-morning, by a fox who had gnawed through the wire fence over a succession of days without our noticing it and who had popped back to collect his prize once he'd got the hole big enough. We were indoors the whole time and heard nothing. If you let your girls out during the day you need to exercise vigilance, because it only takes a few minutes to lose one or more of your flock. Usually one of the chickens will act as a sort of sentry, letting rip if she sees or hears something, so if you hear one of them start up, it's worth taking a quick look (though quite often they appear to be noisy for no reason at all).

One person I spoke to had approximately 30 hens killed in one night, and the foxes didn't actually take any of them away and eat them; they simply went berserk and killed everything that moved. Regrettably that is the nature of the fox, so you stand to lose an entire flock if a fox gets in, not just one bird.

## Winter and Summer

The different seasons don't make as much difference to the girls as you might think. Depending on where you live, wintry conditions will mean one of three problems: snow, cold or rain.

Snow is only a problem if it's thick enough to stop the girls moving through it properly. My hens, on a snowy day, tend to bounce through it - it's the only way - but don't allow them to struggle through snow for more than a short time; their feathers will become very wet, and this will stop their insulation  feathers from doing their job.

You don't need to worry about their getting cold in winter, because they will have moulted and grown a thicker layer of feathers, which they fluff up for extra insulation, and they will huddle together at night for warmth.

Ventilation is really important to get right. In winter they'll be spending longer hours in their coop and without ventilation it will become damp and lead to respiratory problems for your girls, so never, ever cover the ventilation over. At the same time you must keep down draughts, by making sure you shut their pophole door at night. Because they'll be in the house for longer they will also need it kept cleaner, so a bit of 'pooh-picking' each morning will be helpful, to remove the worst of the mess and keep a healthier house for the girls to live in. The more you do this, the less likely it is that parasites can move in.

Over winter it's tempting to think that you need to put a snug cover on the henhouse, but this is dangerous: red mites and other pests haven't gone away in winter - they'll just use a cover over the roof as a handy bolthole until spring.

*A suitable heat lamp for a shed*

If their henhouse is very large, perhaps a converted shed, they may need a heat lamp suspended from the ceiling, well out of reach. I know of one person who had one of these and noticed that there seemed to be a faint smell in her henhouse. Her flock were cuddling together directly underneath the lamp, and were almost cooking themselves, so she had to shorten the flex to the lamp.

Cold is less of a problem if hens can stay comparatively dry. It's tempting to think that they need warming up somehow, but don't forget they're tucked up in feather duvets of their own, so they're not feeling the cold in the way that we would. In extremely cold weather it may help to smear some petroleum jelly over their wattles and combs to protect them from frostbite.

They will keep themselves warm by eating perhaps ten per cent more than usual, so make sure they can always get to their food, especially as their day outside is shorter. Do, however, keep a weather eye out for rodents, attracted by the food.

If it's very icy weather you must check their water at least a couple of times a day. Whatever the weather, it's vital to make sure chickens have plenty of water. There are commercial gadgets available to sit under a water dispenser and warm it slightly but we've found it's best to empty the water dispenser on icy evenings, to save it from freezing overnight, and then fill it with warm water each morning and put it back out. Starting with warmer water should help prevent its freezing for as long as possible, but you must check it throughout the day in case it ices over. Hens do not like iced water!

Really, rain is the main problem. Hens and mud mix rather too well - they end up walking around an inch taller, on a thick slick of mud - and, as with snow, if their feathers get too wet their insulation layer won't be able to do its job. For rain and snow the solution is shelter: a section of their run or garden where these are kept off by either trees or a tough tarpaulin. If you have a portable house, it could simply be moved into a more sheltered area.

In summer weather they will have moulted the thicker layer of feathers and their insulation should keep them fairly cool, as long as you provide some shade at all times. If no trees provide shade, a tarpaulin will do it. Always ensure that there is plenty of water available. In very hot weather change the water a minimum of once a day. Water that's been left standing in hot weather will have less oxygen in it, so it does need to be replaced regularly.

If you intend to go on holiday, you have to be sure that you have a friend or neighbour prepared to look after the flock, which is no small job, when you consider the fact that they have to be around first thing in the morning to open up the pophole door to let the girls out, and again last thing at night, to close it up. They have to be prepared to check for rodents, top up feed, sweep up spilt feed, replenish water frequently, collect eggs - it's a lot of work to ask someone to do, and if a neighbour isn't available to do it you may need to sort out a housesitter for the duration, so they're on hand when needed.

An alternative is to find a local establishment that takes in chickens while people are on holiday. Prices vary, and this may not be a feasible option. Before handing over your hens you need to be sure that the place is run to high standards and that your girls will be well cared for. You may also need to bear in mind that bringing your flock into contact with other people who handle chickens could lead to an invasion of parasites, so there's a lot to consider before packing your suitcase.

# CHAPTER FOUR

## FEEDING

'Grass, grain, greens and grit'. That's the mantra we were given when we decided to keep chickens. Like simpletons, we believed that was all there was to it.

We bought a mixture of layers mash and pellets, and thought we'd done all that was needed. We hadn't really thought about the fact that humans only need vegetables and grains to survive and yet, given a choice, we'll always pick chips, steak and a chocolate pudding.

For a kick off they refused to touch the pellets. We'd been assured that they would make the switch to pellets without a fuss but, as we were beginning to discover, chickens have personalities and they could be just as obstinate as any human. Essentially they picked out the mash and left us to throw away the pellets. Now we just have a feed bin filled with mash, corn and grit. Despite this, most other people I spoke to have their hens eating pellets without any problems. (I bet their kids never answer back or tramp mud across the carpets, either.)

We are lucky to live at a time when chicken feed is a simple thing to buy. Years ago, it was something everybody had to make up for themselves, using complicated formulae for nutritive ratios of cellulose, minerals, carbohydrates, oils, nitrogen and water.

Chicken farmers had to calculate the feed according to whether it was for heat and energy production, egg-laying or what was called 'flesh-forming' and birds would be given feed twice a day, with a measured amount per bird. They were fed oats, potatoes, maize, bran, buckwheat, meat scraps, pea meal, clover, hay and even horse flesh and ground bones!

After the First World War people began to realize that allowing birds unlimited access to feed all day did not mean that they would overeat, but that they were able to keep themselves topped up all day, and this system gave the shyer birds a fair chance at the food. Fortunately this system is now the usual method, whether in farms or back gardens.

It seems to be hard-wired into our consciousness that chickens are fed kitchen scraps. This is a piece of common knowledge that must have been imbibed from our parents or grand-parents, because it is almost universally held. It is, however, quite wrong.

In years gone by it was not only acceptable and legal to feed scraps to chickens, but actually necessary. Chicken feed was not really available and in wartime it would have been considered absolutely unacceptable to waste scraps that could be given to livestock. Times, though, have changed.

DEFRA is the acronym for the snappily-titled Department for Environment, Food and Rural Affairs and their remit is to help farmers operate efficiently and ensure the welfare of farmed animals. Not, on the surface, phrases which are likely to attract the attention of the average back garden chicken keeper. Despite this, according to a gentlemen I contacted at DEFRA, "rules for anyone who intends to keep poultry [...] apply to smallholders such as keepers in gardens". Thus, those of us with half a dozen chickens are expected to trawl through such gems as "poultry welfare at slaughter", or "farm fires and animal welfare" or "biosecurity measures for poultry farmers".

It's frankly not an easy piece of information to track down, but essentially, it boils down to this: even though you don't have to register with DEFRA if you keep fewer than 50 chickens, and even though the majority of hen keepers don't sell their eggs or eat the meat, they are still expected to feed their girls as if they were Farmer Brown with 200 acres. And that means no scraps from food prepared within the human environment of the kitchen, because it can lead to salmonella in the eggs. Salmonella is a bacterium that can cause disease in animals and people and, according to DEFRA, is one of the most significant causes of food poisoning in humans.

Feed is available as pellets or layers mash (or crumbles, which is generally used for battery hens).

When you first bring home point of lay chickens these may not be used to feeding on pellets, so you might need to mix the pellets in with mash to start with and gradually put more and more pellets into the mix until they are used to them. Pellets and mash are the same food, just in different forms, so if your chickens don't fancy pellets, it doesn't really matter, although some people find the pellets less messy than mash.

If you're rehoming battery hens you can't just launch them straight into pellets, because they may not recognize them as food. You can, if you wish, continue to feed them on crumbles, but they will probably cope well with layers mash.

Grass is an obvious part of a chicken's diet. It provides fibre and vitamins, and greens of all kinds do the same. By allowing both where possible the girls will have access to greenstuffs all year round and this will vary their diet and just make life more interesting for them.

Grit is essential, not because of its nutritive value to a bird, but because they have gizzards instead of teeth, to grind food. Pebbles, grit and other indigestible objects collected while foraging provide the grinding action necessary. If you keep your chickens in a run, particularly if it's a concrete area, make sure they have unlimited access to poultry grit.

## The No-Nos

Some people do go to the fairly extreme (not to say OCD) length of setting up a shed in their garden with a little gas burner in it and cook up some food for them there. But because most people live in the real world, and because most have never even *considered* the fact that they shouldn't feed scraps, this is just a selection of some of the foods that some people are giving their hens:

- grated cheese
- breadcrumbs
- porridge
- rice
- the skins off jacket potatoes

- boiled or mashed potatoes
- pasta and spaghetti
- ham sandwiches
- sausages
- raisins and sultanas
- Christmas pudding
- doughnuts
- birthday cake
- sage and onion stuffing (a bit mean?)
- and finally … erm … chicken! Though, given that farmers used to feed meat and bones to poultry, perhaps this isn't as extraordinary as I thought

One lady I heard of easily topped the informal poll I'd started for 'most unwise thing to feed chickens' by feeding live maggots to hers. Maggots, you see, can reach the stomach alive. It was after her eighth hen mysteriously died that she went to a vet to find out why. Despite this, some websites will recommend feeding live maggots to a hen with an impacted crop, to deal with the blockage of food *(see p.55)*.

If your chickens have free rein around the garden, do try to ensure that they are not eating blades of very long grass, perhaps in areas the mower won't reach, because these can become trapped in the crop, causing a blockage *(see p. 55)*.

## A Safe Compromise

Luckily there are ways of providing some fun food without breaking rules or endangering anyone (or unintentionally killing off your flock). Most people have found that fruit and vegetables are big hits with their chickens: they give them grapes, sweetcorn, strawberries, apples, plums, lettuce, cabbage, cauliflower leaves, broccoli leaves; none of which need go near the kitchen at all, if you can take it straight from the garden or allotment for them. As with long grass, though, do check that you're not giving them the tough centre stalks off cauliflower or cabbage leaves, as these can block the crop, as well.

If your girls are in a run, they'll really enjoy a bunch of greenery hung up for them to peck at. If you've top-fenced the run, it's easy to put a metal hook on the fencing and attach some string to it, with a collection of lettuce leaves, grass or even herbs. It makes eating a lot more fun, and will exercise their minds and bodies, as they jump up and down to grab the greens.

An excellent source of natural food for your flock will be insects, which doesn't just benefit the chickens, but your garden, too. If you have a large enough run to give them old logs for perching on, you'll find that these will attract insects, too, adding to your flock's food sources and fun, as they hunt amongst the wood. Ours love to help while we're weeding or digging, because our flock will fight over any snails we find, too. (Our kitchen garden is getting known as a tough gig for a snail.) And no amount of sweet reason, fencing or shouting at them will persuade our hens that rhubarb leaves are poisonous. They all appear to thrive on them.

It seems that most hens, given the chance, will nick dog or cat food, but wild bird food is a safe extra: ours hang about underneath

*They may try for the cat's dinner, but don't let them actually eat it*

the bird table, waiting for the starlings to knock some food down for them.

The leaves from fruit trees and raspberry bushes are often welcomed by the girls, but don't feed them rhubarb leaves: these are poisonous (despite the fact that our flock has always nicked the rhubarb leaves, with no apparent problems, I still wouldn't actually feed them to chickens).

It's not a good idea to give them extras or treats every time you go outside. I knew one elderly gentleman who kept two chickens and was in the habit of putting out raisins and breadcrumbs for them every single time he went outside. Chickens may not be Brains of Britain but they certainly know how to work out that food is in the offing, and since they were able to roam around the garden at all times, this meant that every time he approached the back door the chickens mobbed him.

Since he was elderly he was in real danger of tripping up when they did this, especially as they were creating a slippery slick of - well, let's call it guano - across the path. Feeding the girls like this is not only bad for their health, in giving them food they shouldn't be having, but it also caused a real problem for the owner, who began to feel trapped inside his own house.

The chickens must not expect treats every time they see you, and should have to work for their food, in order to make their lives more interesting, and keep them healthier. They will have feed available all day, so they don't need any treats. However, there is one occasion when I do give them a treat they expect: when I've let them out into the main garden and want to get them back in. They do know that if they go inside their run there'll be something in it for them, and it's the best way to lure them back in without trouble.

Chickens, however, never fail to surprise you. One day I heard a commotion in the hen run and found them dashing madly all over the run, fighting over a mouse, which had been caught while stealing their feed!

Chickens clearly like as wide a variety of diet as we do, though personally I'd turn down sushi mouse.

# CHAPTER FIVE

## Illnesses and Other Troubles

### Vets

Many people make a fundamental error when they need a vet for their chicken: they go to the same vet that cares for their cat or dog. In veterinary medicine, just as in human medicine, there are specialists and the average High Street vet doesn't necessarily know anything about poultry. I've heard of vets giving birds x-rays and injections for all sorts of things, simply because they don't know about birds, but want to try to help. It's a really good idea to seek out your nearest poultry vet *before* you need them, rather than in a panic later, if something befalls one of your flock.

I should add here that you will find no photographs in this chapter: partly because photographing a chicken when in distress is not my favourite occupation, but mainly because a chapter full of photographs of parasites and other nasties is extremely off-putting. You do need to be aware of problems that could occur, and be on the look-out for them, but don't be alarmist: most of the time your chickens will be happy and healthy, and with luck you will never need this chapter. If you ever do need a little more information, I would suggest that you don't start trawling around the internet: ten minutes of this can convince you that there isn't a single healthy chicken in the entire world! Your library will stock other books with detailed information on illnesses and infestations or you can call the farm or breeder who sold you the hens in the first place, because they will almost certainly have help and practical advice for you, without the scare tactics. If your farmer or breeder isn't helpful, that's a very good warning for you. I would avoid that source in future for more hens and go somewhere else.

The other good source of information is your vet, of course, but this is advice you will have to pay for.

## Parasites

Unfortunately, however well we try to look after them, there will inevitably be some sort of problem, ranging from the mild and annoying to the fatal. Several of these could be caused by parasites. Parasites are generally spread by wild birds, so keeping hen feed away from somewhere that wild birds can access it is a really good preventative. It's also important to clean out the house thoroughly and regularly, as many parasites will live on discarded feathers and other waste and the more regularly you clean them out the more likely you are to spot a potential problem early, while it's still comparatively easy to deal with.

One of the best ways for chickens to deal with parasites is to dust bathe frequently, so try to ensure that they have somewhere to do this. If it can be somewhere that wild birds don't access that would be a bonus, though it's just about impossible to achieve this in most gardens. In addition it can be helpful to ensure (in the nicest way possible) that other hen keepers don't get too close to the flock and its housing, and spread anything their flock may have. (Though quite how you phrase that to a hen-keeping friend without causing offence I really don't know).

One of the worst parasite offenders are the tiny, dark red insects known as red mites. When they appeared one day in our flock's house we bought red mite powder, and dusted each chicken with it, then we put it on their perches, under the swing, where they liked their dust baths, and then we went inside and washed it all off ourselves.

A week later there were more of them. The books we had suggested taking the hen-house into the middle of the garden and hosing it down with a jet spray, and keep on doing it until no more mites appeared. Since we (a) didn't possess a jet spray and (b) my husband had built an immovable hen-house, this wasn't going to work. The next book I consulted suggested moving them into a different area completely (and a fresh house) while the first one was fumigated, but their hen-run is also immovably built and, besides, I could see my husband spending the rest of his days building hen-houses.

There was plenty of information available on the internet – unfortunately, as I mentioned earlier, some of it was rather more graphic than I could have done with. There were also a lot of chat rooms and blogs on the subject. The problem was that, however calmly they started, they all, sooner or later, involved someone writing, "...so we wash our hands and boots in bleach fourteen times a day and make sure we always wear the biohazard suit when approaching the hen-coop..." and I began to suspect that I was listening in to the darker side of hen-keeping.

I consulted my friend Sally, who has kept chickens for years and years and was our local expert. She was never reduced to a blubbering wreck because a few dark red specks were trolling around the chickens' perch, so I went to her.

"Red mites?" she said. "My chickens have never had them."

The next day I opened up the bin to put some rubbish in and three million eyes looked back. Then, in an obsessive manner I had hoped I would never descend to, I started looking over my clothes, to make sure I hadn't got any on me. Then I washed my hands a compulsive few times, and then I did something I should have done before – I telephoned the farm which had sold us the hens. Armed with their helpful advice and some diatomaceous earth and poultry insecticide, we went to war.

The mites can last without chickens for up to ten months, but eventually, on a dust-heap without chickens, they would all die, so the bag went to the dustmen and we burned all the paper, and other waste from the hen-coop. I dragged the bin into the middle of the garden where the sun was full on it. Red mites are like very small vampires – they don't like the light, they suck blood and they don't care for garlic (though I don't think crucifixes bother them too much). I poured some bleach into the bin and filled it with boiling water.

We put yet more red mite powder on the chickens and kept them out of their house, while my husband took all the perches and their supports out, and took the nest boxes apart. We scrubbed everything thoroughly with strong bleach, left it out for the sun to dry, then at twilight - which is when any remaining mites would appear - we soaked the house with the poultry insecticide and coated it with diatomaceous earth. Then we let the girls back in.

Diatomaceous earth is formed of tiny crystalline particles which can attach to the mites and attack their outer coating, which is normally impervious. This allows the poultry insecticide in to do its work. We were advised that this method never fails. So far we would agree.

Scaly leg mites are another pest. These are small, burrowing mites which, as the name suggests, get under the scales on a chicken's legs, causing irritation and swelling. There are proprietary solutions which can be used on the birds, though some people prefer to cover the girls' legs with Vaseline, suffocating the mites, and then coating their perches with cooking oil, to trap any others. I can't resist the mental image of all the chickens swaying about on the perch, or slipping round and hanging upside down, but apparently it works. There are, however, commercial treatments for scaly leg mites which are formulated from natural products and are organic.

Fleas and lice are another set of parasites that could cause concern. If a chicken looks listless, is feeding less regularly, has a pale comb, stops laying, starts pulling feathers, or has bald spots, it could well be fleas or lice. If you pick up the hen and study the base of her feathers, particularly near the vent, you may spot them scurrying away. Do note, though, that chicken lice are specific to hens, so humans cannot catch them.

Diatomaceous earth and poultry insecticide work well on all these parasites, but if you prefer natural remedies try products that contain pyrethrin, a natural insecticide, which is sometimes used in animal shampoos. Birds can be shampooed in a similar way to dogs, but absolutely must not be allowed to stay wet, as they may become ill. To find out how to do this, see p. 58.

Coccidiosis is another illness caused by parasites, which can result in very loose liquid droppings, often with blood in them. This will require drugs from the vet to clear up. The best way to avoid this is good cleaning generally and particularly in keeping the feed and water clean and the area dry. This parasite thrives in humid conditions.

Worms are another parasite which can affect chickens, and there are two varieties, unfortunately: one lives in the gut, the other in the windpipe. Both can be controlled by worming the chickens every three months with a proprietary treatment

## Impacted or Sour Crop

Impacted crop is a very serious problem, which once affected one of our flock. The phrase "rarer than hens' teeth" refers to the fact that hens don't actually have any at all, so they eat grit to grind up their food in the crop, which is situated at the base of the neck, and which does the job of breaking food down. If the crop gets blocked, though, they will essentially starve to death if left untreated. This can be caused by a bird accidentally trying to eat something left lying around, like string or plastic, or just by eating very long grass, so don't allow birds to wander into long grass areas (*see Feeding*).

If a chicken is looking very miserable, and has a pale comb and is failing to eat – though perhaps trying to – this could well be the problem. Unless you're extremely confident about dealing with this, it is a job best left to the experts, because the food in the crop must be gently removed and the bird can be badly hurt or choke to death during this process if you don't know what you're doing.

It can help to feed the affected bird cider vinegar, which also helps to break down food, making it harder to block the crop. Adding a little to their water occasionally is a good preventative. In addition some websites will recommend feeding live maggots to a hen with an impacted crop, to deal with the blockage of food. Personally I would never do this, having heard about some of the other results of feeding maggots, but perhaps as a short-term solution it's feasible, if you keep an eye on the hen in question and get to her early enough.

Sour crop may present similar symptoms, but this is caused by a yeast infection in the crop, most generally thought to be caused by mouldy food or incorrect feeding with items that shouldn't be in their diet. It can be difficult to determine whether the problem is an impacted crop or a sour crop, but both are serious, so the best action would be to get her to the vet.

If a hen has had to be treated by the vet she will probably have to be kept in isolation for a short period afterwards. This can be tricky. Very few people keep spare henhouses in their gardens so in our case, when one of our birds developed an impacted crop she got an optimistic 'blanket in a box' arrangement in the shed. After a week of seclusion in there, with visits every day to massage her crop and ensure that she was feeding and drinking well, we decided that she must be feeling better when we caught her peeping out of the window at us, while clearly balancing on some paint pots. The shed was liberally coated with a generous mixture of spilt grain, spilt water and chicken pooh, which proved to have the adhesive qualities of good concrete. One treatment by the vet, though, had been enough, and she was fit and well for the rest of her time with us, dying finally of old age.

## Egg Bound Chickens

This is fortunately fairly rare, but if a bird seems distressed and keeps visiting the nesting box without actually laying, she may be having difficulty with an exceptionally large egg. If she's still distressed after some hours, it may be necessary to take action, either by gently holding her in a bowl of water which is slightly more than lukewarm, to ease her muscles, and let the egg through, or by gently massaging her to ease it through, but as with everything else, if in doubt, consult the vet, as if the egg breaks it could cause an infection.

## Accidents

Burns and scalds are rare and the feathers afford a lot of protection, but a bird who is seriously burned may need to be put down straight away. It's difficult to dress wounds beneath feathers, but a minor burn or scald could be treated this way and the hen kept isolated for a while. Again, this is best dealt with by a trip to the vet.

Injuries to the comb and wattles should be bathed with warm water and treated with antiseptic, but any serious wound needs veterinary care.

Similarly, broken or fractured bones should be dealt with professionally or the bird put down, but actually birds' bones mend fairly easily if they're not too old and the vet gets to it quickly.

## Bumble-Foot

This is a swollen area under the foot, which gradually hardens and becomes very painful. This is usually caused by the hen having to jump down constantly from a high perch onto a hard floor. If this develops, take the bird to the vet, and she may have to be kept isolated for a few days to let it heal.

The best solution is not to let it happen in the first place, by ensuring that the perches are a comfortable height for the flock and that they are landing on a softer surface.

## Moulting

Something that isn't an illness but can sometimes seem like one, is moulting. Birds need to moult, just as cats or horses change the thickness of their coats according to season. You can expect to see the hens doing this a couple of times a year as the weather cools in autumn or heats up in spring.

Most of the time you'll only be aware they're moulting when you see a lot of feathers lying about in the house or run, as though there's been a pillow fight in the dorm, and you might find fewer eggs. This is because all their energy is going into producing new feathers rather than eggs. There's no doubt they do look a bit ridiculous when they lose their tail feathers and the softer ones on their bottoms, but mostly you can safely ignore all that.

Very occasionally moulting can take a more extreme form – birds can look very miserable, or downright ill. They might stay in the nesting box all day; they might not eat; they may look very lethargic; they may be ignored by the rest of the flock and sit alone; they may even appear not to be able to walk, which is very alarming to see, but if a chicken's comb is a good, red colour and she has an alert look it probably isn't a parasite infestation: she could simply be moulting.

I have heard of people rushing chickens to the vet only to find it was simply a bad moult, but there is always the chance that it is something more serious, so in these circumstances it's best just to keep a close eye on them and ensure that your chicken is getting food and water. If after a few days there isn't any improvement, it's worth asking your poultry vet's opinion.

In any case, it can only help a hen to have some feed supplements to help get their energy back. There are several commercial products available, but we find that putting apple cider vinegar or a couple of garlic bulbs into their water is very good at keeping a lot of problems at bay. Feeding a moulting or generally unhappy bird some live yoghurt is recommended, as it provides some 'good bacteria' to boost their immune systems.

## Washing Chickens

This is not something everybody knows how to do, but I do. The reason I had to find out is that one of our flock had been moulting and had a particularly grubby bottom, so it was decided at a family meeting, which I was not allowed to attend, that she should be washed by hand. My hand, to be precise.

The method is as follows:-

First beg, borrow or – if absolutely necessary buy - some baby shampoo, or dog shampoo containing pyrethrin. Then select your chicken. I've made it sound easier than it is, of course. The phrase "select your chicken" cannot fully convey the difficulties inherent in picking one bird out from an excitable flock without the use of a large net, a sheepdog or a lasso. The chicken you actually want to get hold of will be discovered nonchalantly ignoring you in the deepest and most inaccessible recesses of their run.

However, some tortuous time later you will be ready to commence operations. Rubber gloves are a must for this job. You will need a shallow bowl of warm (not hot) water with a drop of shampoo in to stand the chicken in. They're not keen on this, so a fair amount will end up everywhere except where it's wanted, and it's best to be pretty quick about it. If you're treating them for parasites, you need to be gentle, thorough AND quick, which is even more difficult. Once you've finished, quickly rinse off the soapy water.

You will now be standing in the garden with a wet chicken (and the phrase "madder than a wet hen" is very well chosen indeed).

Carry her into your kitchen/conservatory/shed or wherever you have an electricity supply, plonk her down onto a heap of newspaper, plug in the hairdryer and start (keeping the dryer on a low heat, or a decent distance from the chicken so it doesn't burn her). Now here's the interesting bit: chickens adore hairdryers. They won't budge while it's on. They settle down, smooth their feathers, shut their eyes and – well, I can only assume she was doing some sort of yoga meditation. I had enormous difficulty in getting her to move once I'd done. However, fun though this is for the chicken, it's still something you wouldn't want to be doing regularly.

# CHAPTER SIX

## BEHAVIOUR

### Single Hens

Chickens are naturally flock creatures, probably because a flock provides greater security from predators. The size of the group and its ability to perform natural behaviour are important for hens' welfare. Domestic fowl naturally live in small groups.

Different people need different numbers of hens. Some are just looking for a couple only, to lay the odd egg and be interesting pets. Some are after four or five chickens, and some want a much larger flock, to allow for eating the meat as well. The one thing to avoid is for a chicken to be alone. They are creatures that need the company of a flock, and if other birds aren't available they will seek the company of humans, instead.

A neighbour of ours has found herself, quite by accident, with a single chicken, called Fanny. Because of her age they made the decision that it would be less distressing for Fanny not to have to cope with a new chicken (and, frankly, less distressing for a new chicken not to have to cope with Fanny) and just to leave her to live out the rest of her life alone. Well, I say alone …

Fanny, you see, is an unusual chicken. Her owner has a conservatory with a lovely view out to the garden, which allows Fanny, strolling around the flowerbeds, to keep her eye on the humans and see if anything interesting is happening. If it is, she knocks on the back door with her beak until they let her in.

The family dog, settled quietly on her favourite chair in the conservatory, would get booted off by the chicken and would have to take refuge in the house. Actually Fanny had her own chair, but always preferred the dog's one. Not too many hens have their own seating.

Fanny also likes snuggling up to humans, while sitting on their laps, shoving her head under their arm until they stroke her. It's exactly like having a lap full of cat, except for the wriggling and the feathers.

She, though, is an exception. Fanny's lucky to have a family who spend a lot of time with her, but it's not generally speaking a good idea for hens to be on their own.

## Nesting Behaviour

In the wild a hen will usually move away from the rest of the flock to find a secluded nesting place, either as protection from predators or from bad weather conditions and in domestic flocks chickens like a bit of peace and quiet when laying. It's because of this that you will usually need more than one nest box and these will need to be inside, where it's quiet. This won't prevent them all from wanting the same nest box, but at least you'll know they've got the option. Some people prefer to keep former battery hens, and give them a chance to live a more natural life, but research suggests that these hens may not be able to switch to using nest boxes, but will want to lay outside.

For some reason chickens do seem to decide arbitrarily that one nest box is the favourite and completely ignore the other, which is why you need to supply at least two for them. We have found that sometimes they will suddenly switch to the other nesting box for no reason apparent to us and stick with that for months before suddenly deciding that the first one is preferable again. Whichever they prefer, they won't use the 'other' nest box if the favourite is occupied; they simply fuss about to make the occupying hen get out.

## Foraging

Chickens prefer areas with trees and tend to avoid bright sun, so a covered area is a must for them, whether it's natural tree cover or just a tarpaulin or wooden boards. Be cautious with certain breeds, though, which can fly a little better than others and love roosting in trees (*see Breeds*). Chickens will always want to be able to see the approach of predators, whether it's a fox or the neighbour's cat and you will probably find that one of the flock will stay on high alert, keeping an eye out while the others forage.

Most of their time outside will be spent pecking the ground, even when they're not hungry and food is available freely at all times. The rest of the time they'll be dust bathing, grazing and scratching, depending on the weather.

This foraging helps give the hens something to do, helps keep aggressive behaviour at bay and is far better for them than being cooped up in close confinement, being closer to their natural behaviour patterns. It also helps the gardener, because ranging around the garden means their droppings are scattered over the garden, doing a lot of good to the soil, and they are keeping pests down.

## Resting and Sleeping

Chickens are basically controlled by the pattern of light and dark, so at dusk they will look for perches.

With our first flock we had enormous trouble getting any of them to leave the house in the morning and spent ages trying to persuade them out. This involved one of our daughters leaning in through the back of the house and trying to urge them out through the pophole door. We should have just left them to it, because they all appeared to be clinging on inside. Maybe they were using Velcro.

Once they were out, and as it started to grow dark, we waited for the moment when they would trot up their little ladder and take themselves back to bed – and they didn't seem to want to. Again, we wasted a good hour trying to catch each one, get her through the pophole door, and then catch the next. Their run is quite large, but it's not large enough for four people to dodge about in with chickens under their arms, trying to persuade them to go to bed.

Of course, we were being impatient. In fact it's light levels that tell the girls when it's time to get up, not scary humans with a deadline, and similarly at night, when the light level drops just enough, they will take themselves to bed, and then they're out like a light. Well, apart from Erica.

Erica is our special needs chicken – though we didn't know this when we bought her. She's a speckled hen and after her first day with us my husband went to lock the house down for the night and found all of them tucked up indoors – apart from Erica, who was sound asleep on the outside perch. My husband was not too happy at having to put a chicken to bed (not in our bed, you understand – having a chicken asleep on your bedpost could be thought weird).

We'd only had her for a fortnight, when we heard a lot of commotion outside at dusk, as they were going to bed. We discovered Erica slumped, dead, in the doorway, with all the others trampling her in their efforts to get inside. It was quite upsetting to lose a bird so soon after getting her, but when I went into the run to retrieve her body she stood up, glared at me, and then went in to bed. We clearly had a chicken who thought she was a cat and could sleep anywhere.

Once they work out that they can sleep indoors, you will find that they are totally silent at night, because hens essentially shut down when it's dark.

Birds will also sleep during the day (usually as a flock) and they tend to prefer doing this in a sunny spot, where the whole group will settle, apart from the 'guard' chicken. This way of settling together only generally occurs when they are resting. When they're active, they usually like a bit of 'personal space'.

## Introducing New Chickens to the Flock

Losing a chicken to old age, or a fox, or illness, is often the moment when we need to buy another and it can be a bit fraught to introduce youngsters to an established flock. It's usually worst when you first introduce new ones to the first flock, because they've never had to cope with the situation before and can react badly. After the first time they kick up a lot less fuss.

It's generally best to put new chickens into the henhouse and close the door, to allow them peace and quiet when they first settle in. As dusk approaches open the pophole door up and allow the older ones in to sleep. They won't like finding strangers in there, but they won't start a battle at bedtime.

Another advantage in locking the newbies into the house to start with is that if you release them straight into their run they will have no idea where to go to sleep. However, there can be a certain amount of aggression towards new members of a flock (*see Bullying*).

In the morning it might take a while for the newbies to stick their beaks out and investigate, and the shyer ones will hang around indoors for even longer, but eventually they will leave the house.

People talk about a 'pecking order' and the phrase originates with a flock of chickens. Quite literally they establish who is who in their flock in order of importance, by pecking, and new members of the flock have to endure a certain amount of this.

It looks pretty awful to a human, but it's vital that they be allowed to do it. If a human intervenes and splits up the chickens, to allow the youngsters a breathing space, it will do a lot of harm, because they will never integrate properly and will always have problems with each other. If you keep them apart you will essentially end up with two flocks. It shouldn't last too long, but if it goes on, it could be a case of bullying (*see below*).

## Bullying

Within a flock subordinate hens can often be bullied. The two words "chickens" and "aggression" are not generally something we imagine belonging together, and it can be distressing to see one hen apparently being bullied by another (or the entire flock). There can be several reasons for it and it's important to work out why it's happening in order to deal with it the right way.

If the victims are newbies, it could simply be a matter of the established flock letting the young ones know their place. In this case the hens soon settle down and within a couple of days they'll usually have taught the youngsters who's the boss.

Each bird in a small, stable flock, such as exists in the typical back garden, will be high or low ranking, but if the pecking isn't happening because of new additions to the flock you need to look for another reason.

One reason for bullying can be the physical sizes of the various hens. It's important to ensure, for instance, that you don't put bantams in with larger birds, while some breeds are just naturally less aggressive. Buff Orpingtons, for instance, are generally very timid and quiet, despite their size, so these should not be put in with other, more aggressive, breeds, if possible.

Some breeds, however, are physically smaller than others, and would be at a disadvantage, so it's important not to subject smaller birds to this sort of treatment, but keep to similar sized varieties. However, if it continues for longer than a few days with newbies, or if it's happening in an established flock, it could have some other cause. It's worth checking to see that they have sufficient feed and water and you may need to provide extra feeders in another area, to stop the bigger or higher status chickens keeping a timid one out.

Constant feather pecking, if they eat the feathers, could be down to calcium deficiency, so a supplement could be useful, and make sure that there is plenty of oyster shell available in their feed. Nesting boxes can be the cause of a few fights, too. It's particularly a problem if you have a broody hen, who won't relinquish the box to any of the others. Hens don't queue. Allow your girls at least one nest box for every three to four hens.

More space in their run gives a bullied hen some room to manœuvre, too, and extra outdoor perching places can provide safe places for the timid ones to hide. Some old tree branches are great for this.

Just like us, hens can also be bored, so allowing them to range out of their pen if possible is a good idea and so is hanging up vegetables or pecking blocks for them. If they're having to work to get some food it keeps their minds off pecking the others and keeps them busy. Even hanging up old CDs as a distraction can work.

If a hen *is* being pecked by a bully you need to get her out to recover and perhaps isolate the bully for a few days, or the rest of the flock may begin to join in. Feather peck spray is also available and may help. If left unchecked, a bullied chicken could be pecked to death, so if a hen is bleeding remove her immediately.

A good method is to keep the isolated hen where she can see the others, but they can't reach her. If the bullies can be kept in while the victim is allowed to free range, she will feel safer and they will not feel as though they've been rewarded for their antisocial behaviour. In these circumstances it may be best for the bullied hen to sleep separately from the flock, as well.

If this doesn't work, try removing the bully instead, for a few days. When she's put back into the flock she will have dropped to the bottom of the pecking order and shouldn't cause any more problems.

If all else fails, you will either need to remove the bully or the victim permanently, perhaps to another hen keeper, or bring in a cockerel to keep order.

Fortunately aggression is very unlikely to occur if you start your girls off with the best conditions. Good food and some interesting things to do will usually lead to a contented flock.

(In our case, we have a hen who is fascinated by my husband's trousers, and follows him whenever he goes outside, but maybe we've just got the weird flock.)

## Temperament

A good rule of thumb is that the heavier, dual-purpose type of breeds that lay brown eggs will be much friendlier than light breeds that lay white eggs. For example, Buff Orpingtons, Wyandottes, Sussex, Rhode Island Reds, Silkies and Welsummers all tend to be much more docile and happy to be handled than some pure breeds. Orpingtons especially have a reputation for being sweet-tempered.

This is mainly important when children are involved in caring for chickens, but it's as well to bear in mind that if you are keeping dual-purpose breeds for slaughter as well as egg production, children won't appreciate the idea of eating a creature they've named and petted.

Plenty of handling will improve life for the birds and make it much easier to check their health and get them out to the vet.

## Aberrant Behaviour

Essentially, aberrant behaviour is usually a sign of something being wrong. A bird may be ill, it may have parasites; it may be egg bound, or distressed because it's being bullied by a bigger bird. Whatever the reason the situation needs to be monitored, and all possible causes investigated. Is there plenty of food? Can all the birds access it easily, or is one of them being kept away by the others? Do they have plenty of fresh water? Can they all get to a nesting box without trouble? Is one visiting the nest-box too often without laying? Are her feathers looking okay? Are there problems with her legs? Is her comb a good colour, or is it pale? Is the bird listless, or just sitting around? Is she staying indoors all the time? It could simply be that a new bird has been introduced to the flock and it or the original flock are unhappy about it. It could be that a fox has been sniffing around, unknown to you. Keep an eye on the situation and, especially if it is only one hen that's having trouble, don't wait too long before consulting a vet, if you're unsure what the problem is.

## Broody Hens

If one of your girls fails to put in an appearance after laying, but stays in the nest box, perhaps making strange noises, and being unwilling to be touched or moved, she may well be broody. Some types of hens are more likely than others to do this. Only two of our hens have ever done this, and they were both the same breed, Rhode Rock.

This is not an illness, but if they persist in staying indoors they won't be getting food and water and may become weaker, all of which will put them more at risk of attack by parasites, or other problems. It can also cause trouble with the other hens, especially if she's in the nesting box which they consider the favourite, and they want her to get out. As a rule of thumb, the heavier breeds, like Rhode Island Red, Light Sussex or Plymouth Rock are more prone to broodiness than lighter breeds, like Leghorns.

Broodiness is triggered by an elevated body temperature, so some owners will take their hen out of the nest box and put her into a bowl of cool water (not cold), but an alternative approach is to allow her two to three days in there, perhaps with dummy eggs, so that you can take out the real ones without upsetting her. After that she needs to be persuaded out, so that she feeds. Just stepping out of the nest box will cool her a little and she may give it up all on her own. Generally hunger will drive them out in the end, anyway, but, as with most things, you will need to keep an eye on her.

Of course, broodiness is only a problem if it's misplaced. If you're rearing chicks and need a hen to sit on a clutch of eggs, this is a positive feature and very useful, though it's often more reliable to use an incubator.

## Human and Animal Interaction

Chickens are generally not too worried by dogs and cats, as long as the dog or cat don't try to start anything. It's in the nature of some dogs to try to chase them, but dogs can be trained to understand that the chickens are residents in the garden, so if they are introduced to the birds gradually they will usually be fine. Cats, of course, are a different matter. Cats may be trainable when it comes to big budget Hollywood films, but in a back garden? No. We have a cat who occasionally tries it on with them, but the flock generally works together to intimidate her, so she backs down. A solo chicken might not be safe, since cats really won't leave something alone if it looks feathery and fun to taunt. Our cat is much more circumspect now, though, about stalking chickens through our kitchen garden, because when she tried it in the past one of them went for her, and she high-tailed it into the kitchen, to hide behind me.

The biggest interaction problems usually start with humans. We have our own ideas about what's supposed to happen, and it doesn't always coincide with what our pets think.

Even though they have a very large run, we try to let our chickens out as often as possible, but this wasn't without difficulties in the early days. Originally we tried chicken-herding - a bit like *One Man and his Dog*. We didn't have a sheepdog available, and the cat wasn't interested, so it was all down to one of our daughters, who was supposed to keep an eye on them, and urge them back into the run when it was getting dark.

Like a lot of apparently good ideas, we soon abandoned it, much to my daughter's relief, but that first time they decided that going indoors just wasn't as interesting as being able to dig up the raspberries, pooh on the lawn, and scare the cat. As it became darker, I waited in vain for the moment when they'd all decide it was time to knock off for the day and trot back home and while I was standing in the lighted kitchen watching them, realization finally dawned: they were never going to decide it was getting dark, because it wasn't. Our lights were on. All they were doing was circling gradually closer and closer to the house. I was providing floodlit grazing for chickens. So I turned the light off. I had a totally blacked-out garden and four hens loose out there somewhere, as visible in the gloom as black cats in a coal-hole.

My daughter and I cautiously stepped down the path, waiting for the bwerk! of a stepped-on chicken, but all was silent. Clearly, they were all holding their breath. I put the kitchen light back on and eventually my daughter and I cornered them all, but there's no doubt our hens came off better in that contest.

## Gardens

One aspect of their behaviour that can cause more anguish than any other is their approach to a garden. Let loose in a kitchen garden it's not long before soil starts flying in all directions as they scratch at the ground. Anything recently planted will come up with the worms they're after and trying to persuade them off the patch just sets up a flurry of feathers, with hens lurching in different directions.

We realized this was going to be a constant problem unless we kept them locked away in their run, which would be a shame, so we decided to be a bit more canny. We began by fencing off the kitchen garden and my husband laboriously built two removable gates that would fit into the remaining areas where two paths went through. He put a lot of effort into it, which was a bit of a shame, as the chickens just went straight over the top instead. My husband took that one personally and he bought a roll of thick wire, so that he could string that along the fence and gates and make them that bit taller, so the hens couldn't quite fly over. It worked, too. Now they just balance on it, like feathery circus performers, and then hop down the other side.

*Tonto doing the chicken version of the high wire act. Old cages keep a plant completely protected.*

Every time my husband starts digging he has at least four chickens clustered round him, eating every worm he turns up and getting in his way. Every time he pots up plants the girls immediately dig them straight up again. And apart from all that, they insist on eating the rhubarb leaves.

Before my husband lost any chance at getting a rhubarb crumble he tried constructing a corral to go around the plants, so that the girls would have nowhere to land if they jumped over. Well, maybe it's just our flock that are so good at balancing. They even have the cheek to try to hide under what's left of the leaves if they see us coming out into the garden, as though we're never going to spot the large feathery things peeking out from under the tattered plants.

Plan C was to put an old rat cage over the rhubarb and that's absolutely the only thing that worked - until the leaves got quite big and poked through the bars. The chickens seemed to be unstoppable. We were in despair, because you can only have so many old rat cages around the garden. We were beginning to get looks from the neighbours.

And then one day, in the middle of a heatwave, when I was upstairs, I looked out at the garden. The plants had survived the earlier misuse and were flourishing, the apple and pear trees were covered in fruit, the raspberries and beans and peas were all doing well, the grass was a lovely green. Then I looked across at all the neighbours' gardens. *Their* grass was brown. In fact everything in the other gardens was wilting, or dead. And I suddenly realized: the chickens *weren't* destroying everything. They had certainly destroyed some things, granted, but they'd also eaten every pest that was out there: the snails that used to destroy our beans; the caterpillars that attacked the brassicas; the ants and the woodlice. In the process they'd scratched at the soil and helped to break it up. And then they'd helpfully poohed everywhere and added some nitrogen to the soil. And when they'd finished doing *that* they'd gone and laid some eggs for us, as well. The only thing left out there that they wouldn't deal with was the slugs, but I suppose you can't have everything.

So now we use spare chicken wire to cover the strawberry plants and to protect the roots around every new plant, and we corral off the tubs like a miniature Colditz, and we make sure we only do any digging or open up the composters when the chickens are away indoors, to give the poor worms a chance to hide themselves. The rest of the time we resign ourselves to a certain amount of minimal damage, in exchange for some really fine pest control. We simply accept that the hens are going to be doing their tightrope walking act and enjoy the show.

I still think the spangly costumes and the balancing stick are overdoing it, though.

# AND FINALLY ...

Keeping chickens is one of those things that people often start almost casually, but surprisingly often the little feathered so-and-so's take over our lives; giving us eggs, but also giving us a lot of entertainment and some fun. They are characters, no less than our cats and dogs and guinea-pigs are characters, and as such they deserve our care and attention.

Happy chicken-keeping!

# INDEX

# ABOUT THE AUTHOR

Lorraine Coverley lives in Essex, England, with her family and six chickens. She has been amusing listeners with her tales of chicken keeping for several years now, in a column, and has written articles on keeping chickens for *Grow Your Own* magazine.
Her other work is available on Amazon, Alfie Dog, Cinnamon Press and Comedy Plays and in magazines.

She really does have a chicken who played dead.

Printed in Great Britain
by Amazon

66005539R00047